Crushing It

CRUSHING IT

Poems | Jennifer L. Knox

Copper Canyon Press
Port Townsend, Washington

Cover art: Larassa Kabel, *Alamo,* 2016, colored pencil on paper,
44½ × 31¾ inches

Copper Canyon Press is in residence at Fort Worden State Park
in Port Townsend, Washington, under the auspices of Centrum.
Centrum is a gathering place for artists and creative thinkers
from around the world, students of all ages and backgrounds,
and audiences seeking extraordinary cultural enrichment.

LIBRARY OF CONGRESS CATALOGING-IN-PUBLICATION DATA
Names: Knox, Jennifer L., 1968– author.
Title: Crushing it : poems / Jennifer L. Knox.
Description: Port Townsend, Washington : Copper Canyon Press, [2020]
Identifiers: LCCN 2020017903 | ISBN 9781556595868 (paperback)
Subjects: LCGFT: Poetry.
Classification: LCC PS3611.N694 C78 2020 | DDC 811/.6—dc23
LC record available at https://lccn.loc.gov/2020017903

98765432 FIRST PRINTING

COPPER CANYON PRESS
Post Office Box 271
Port Townsend, Washington 98368
www.coppercanyonpress.org

For my mother

I am sure the crabs & shrimps join hands and caper about when the tide is coming in and the children have gone home.

Beatrix Potter

CONTENTS

Crushing It

I. Mines

THE MORNING I MET MY NEW FAMILY

A forest of conifers stands upright on the floor
of Fallen Leaf Lake in California's Tahoe Basin,
deposited by millenniums of landslides. Trees 100
feet tall, mummified in icy alpine water, needles
still pristine. Rock-encrusted root-balls weigh
them down, but every now and then one
shoots up like a prehistoric rocket.

                      Everyone else
on the yacht was passed out when Merle Haggard
heard a roar, looked up from the pile of cocaine and saw
a whale-sized Christmas tree erupt from the water,
felt its wake's glittery spray, smelled its piney sap as
it sailed over the deck, hovered a sec, spun, then splatted
back to earth unanchored, yet forever tethered to Merle
and all the naked people stirring on deck, awakened
by this second birth, as "From now on all my friends
are gonna be strangers" blared on repeat.

WOLVERINE SEASON

"Oh, honey, are you okay?"
I asked the woman in the bathroom,
soaking wet as if she'd just emerged
from the shower. "Yeah—maybe too
mush rum on an empty shtomach."
She wiped her mouth with her hand
and left. In the sink, waxy red flecks
of lipstick. "That woman over there
just puked up lipstick in the bathroom!"
I yelled in my friend's ear over
the Black Sabbath tribute band.
"Write a poem about that!"
she yelled back and smiled.
We were up late for a school night—
it was all part of the new regimen.
The documentary I'd just seen about death
said rocking out is actually good for you.
And rocking out to Sabbath? Dude,
we were gonna live, like, forever
on the bones other animals passed up.

MR. BIG

"So I've been reading about this
        police sting operation that's legal
                in Canada and Australia, but not here. The . . . *criminal?*"

            "The *perp!*" B corrects me and takes
                a sip of her macchiato.

"Ha! The *perp!* Yes, so the perp
        brutally murdered his girlfriend and the cops
                couldn't pin it on him so they
                        sent in an undercover man who looked like a real
                                big-shot mafioso type . . ."

                "Mmhm. *Mr. Big,*" B nods.

"Exactly. So Mr. Big gives the perp
        a lot of *important* things to do, run money,
                deliver packages, drive him around,
                        and all the while Mr. Big's telling the perp
                                I can't run things without you, blah blah blah . . ."

                    "Mmhm. Heh."

"Then he says to the perp, *We're taking this business
        to the next level and I want you to run the show, but
                you gotta tell me everything you ever did
                        wrong . . .* I mean . . ."

                    "Idiot."

"Can you imagine someone showing up
        out of nowhere and saying,
                You're just the guy we've been looking for!
                        And you *believe* them?!"

"No, I cannot," B snorts

and I snort.

"Hi," I yip too quickly at a woman walking by
    our bench. It's rare—foot traffic at the end
        of this secluded marble hall, where we've come
        to hide from everyone who
            has, could, and will turn on us.

OLD WOMEN TALKING ABOUT DEATH

When did I become one of them? I used to
roll my eyes at their gory stories: EMTs found
a neighbor at the bottom of her basement steps,
a head-to-toe hematoma. "'Use a cane,' I told her!"
[shrugs]. Grandma and the great-aunts itemized her
injuries. "Poor dear. How long till she was found?"
They told their stories picnicking atop our people
at the cemetery, atop all the men in our family who
died young. The rest disappeared [shrugs] so no stories
for them. These days when I call K, she tells me about
her friends who are dying or have died since we last spoke,
and I feel closer to her, an adult. Yesterday, J filled me in on
M's cancer. "It's baaaad," she whispered. I leaned forward.
M's doctors removed her necrotic uterus through her
abdomen in two jammy black hunks because her insides
had decayed into a sarcomatous tar pit—then her incision
dehisced. I cocked my head. She made a starburst
motion over her belly button. [Ah!] "I've heard that happens
with cancer," I said, grateful Z described the process
to me after her stepmother died. Now I even have a
name for that indignity. Thank God. I hate surprises.

FRIEND OF THE DEVIL

Ron was last seen circling the shelves inside
a QuikTrip near Lutsen. "He seemed lost,"
the clerk said. The gas-pump camera showed
Mary, Ron's wife, slumped down in their car,
but we'll never learn how Ron, 81, with dementia,
managed to get Mary, 79, half-paralyzed,
into the passenger seat. An adrenaline-soaked
feat of strength, or will—must've been
an ugly, grunting driveway dance. On the radio,
their son begs listeners for tips. "They won't last
long without their pills . . ." Then we're back

to the Grateful Dead Hour. "Attics of My Life."
Though I spare you my story about taking a whiz
in the Anaheim Stadium parking lot on acid
back in '87—Petty and Dylan opened—I want to
re-re-retell it to you bad ("No one can see me!"),
I think because my brain's been scrambled by
fear. I watched a documentary about it on TV,

how a crying child left to cry never really stops,
never knows smooth soothing, lives in a state
of unarmored ever-fret until the helplessness
melts, freezes, and flips over in a beat to blackout
rage. So this quiet, loving thing—this glacially
slow forward movement unburdened by burning
and burying us—itches like hell. But you're psyched

to drive to a nice sunny beach on Lake Superior
and get your feet wet like a normal person on vacation.
There's a veil across the screen I perceive.
Your shirt's already off, "Isn't this great!" I stand
there, popping like water dropped in hot lard.

Even if you were as fogged out as Ron, you'd be
solid, no sudden moves. You'd never be compelled
to pull a stunt like he did, but I would.

"I love you," I say inside my head, and back
in the rental car, it comes out: "I know I'm capable
of killing someone for money." "Where do you
come up with this stuff?" you ask, nowhere near
my damage, and turn the radio up before I can
reply, so I sing along with "Ripple" (if you fall,
you fall alone) until what I'm sure will be
bad news interrupts the song.

YOU LOOK AT, NOT THROUGH, THE WINDOW

Old photograph of the woman
who would always be un-
ravelable, a ball of yarn dipped in
glue, thread thick as a cough: bare
legs in black-and-white winter,
scrunched smile cupping a sun-
blind squint. Dad drove her and
her sisters onto the frozen Ohio
and locked them in the car while
he drank with the hoboes. She
never knew what was happening.
Still doesn't. Likes it/hates it.
Same/same. She read books
locked in the bathroom. I'm
trying to land a blame line on her.
I can't. The frame's not her fault.
Gray trees on the far bank loom
like boogeymen.

THE GIFT

You can tell whether a bird has a mate
if there are pinfeathers on its head, new feathers
that start out as stubs full of blood, then enshroud
themselves in a white, scaly coat as they grow.
Preening releases the feather, but a bird can't reach
the top of its own head. A mate preens that spot
unless the bird is alone in a cage. Pinfeathers itch,
so I preen my unpaired birds: wrap them in a towel,
scritch their heads and blow till dandruffy stuff
flutters out. They looked pretty mangy this morning,
I recall, as I stare at the side of my mother's face
from the backseat. How long has it been since I
took her in for a haircut? And her whiskers—she can't
see to shave. We're driving back roads, pointing out
deer and hawks as she *ah*s, before taking her back
to her apartment. Collin calls it "traveling gravel."
She loves it when he drives and I sit in the back
so she can talk as much as she wants. He always
answers her questions. Sometimes I'll go hours
without saying a word while she talks and talks.
When I was little, she'd bring a book to restaurants
and read while I, no doubt, talked and talked. Things
children said weren't interesting to her, she told me,
and family never had to say, "I'm sorry." Yes,
we've hurt each other, but only I've done it
on purpose. Did I tell you she bought me this car?
It's the most generous gift I've ever received.

POSTED: NO FLEDGING IN THE PARKING LOT

Tony's mom, Lulu, knew without thinking,
felt without knowing, that fear kept family
alive, and so sewed only noes and worry into
the lining of their moldy garbage nest. Hugs
felt tight in Tony's jaw, though, and he was
lonely as a tank. Lulu'd later testify the dark
velvet curtain pulled across her brain doubled
as a screen for heartwarming classics like *Lassie*.
She warned him, "That crumpled ball at the foot
of the tree never saw ground coming!" as she
pried open Tony's palm, pressed a pink
pill into it, and shuffled off to the pet shop.
"Thanks, Ma," Tony said, feeling a splinter
where the pill was etching itself into his skin.
"I'll wait here," he informed her blank spot.
A teen wrestling a herd of wobbly carts asked,
"Excuse me, who is that?" and pointed to her
red coat disappearing through double glass doors.
"That's my mother," Tony said. "Well, she's
a real nice lady," the boy replied, pulled a pink
pill from his pocket and popped it in his mouth.
"Sharing is caring," Tony said automatically,
but the words rose from an undiscovered pit
deep in his body—a hidden tiger-trap of love.
"And teamwork makes dream work!" the boy
sang back, his eyelids struggling to stay afloat.

MONOCHROME RAINBOWS

I used to worry a lot about money
(and think about killing myself) too,
but today I'm rich! All because I took
an enormous pill that made me
a financial genius, and now I know
how to do all sorts of Money Things like
a pro but better than a pro (a queen!):
speculate on futures, for example,
and manage risk. *Very* lucrative stuff.
Did you know if you google "APR,"
you get stuff about annual percentage rates—
not *American Poetry Review*? Well, now I do,
and I can make the most incredible spreadsheet:
when I push the mystery button
(which is no longer a mystery to me!)
money shoots out of it, then my eyes,
which no longer see colors other than
green but bees don't either, right?
And they seem happy enough,
in their heavy bodies.

1.   Stop the action.

    1a. Does that include apologizing?

        1b. Because I'm sorry about this poem. I'm so embar-
            rassed. Please forgive me.

3.   Tape pictures of policemen all around the house, especially
        on the refrigerator.

7.   Cheap tops.

49.   Cheap tops.

    ii. Cheap tops that no fit now, nor ne'er will, Captain!

4.   Airline miles, baby [rubs hands together greedily]!

8.   See the future.

9.   To soothe yourself, recite *Ghostbusters*.

    99. Again.

        999. Let's show this prehistoric bitch how we do
            things downtown.

12.   I'm sorry again.

    1221. [mechanic lopes in wiping his oily hands on a rag]
            "Welp, I'm pretty sure you had yourself a full-fledged
            nervous breakdown back there!"

13.   Stop apologizing.

    13a. Right?!? Fuck you! [breaks beer bottle]

        13af. [Steven Seagal-style] Make meeeeeeh.

14–19. Dear reader . . . wanna make out?

27.   Have a sense of humor about your ADHD.

28.   Oh, I can hang! [at policemen] HEY, PIGS! CREEP MY
        FRIDGE MUCH?!?!?! [maniacal laughter, lightning]

38.   Yoo-hoo! Mister DeMille! [lights, sirens, plastic bracelets]

X.   I dance [Bugs Bunny imitating Danny Kaye in *Hot Cross Bunny* (1948)] . . .

    xx. . . . for *you,* dear reader!

        ∞. [hands them the box, they shake it (hint: the bird's dead)]

Y.   See you on the other side, Ray.

Z.   I'm trying to tell myself a different story these days.

    zz. "You're fifty-one years late

        zzz. but I forgive you."

A sudden spotlight floods the black
empty stage. How long have we been
sitting here? Are you, next to me, still
you? Funny how the dark can make you
feel alone—even though people are
all around you—and feel bad, like you
did something dumb. A person (?)
in a panda costume steps from the wings,
strolls center stage, and pulls a cherry
from its pocket. "This is a paycheck,"
it declares, the voice within the head
muffled by fake fur and plastic. "Bullshit,"
you whisper in my ear—whisper because,
I can tell, you're afraid the panda will
hear you. Maybe I should be afraid, too,
but all I feel is bad because the panda thinks
I'm dumb enough to believe its lies. Hey,
maybe it's right! We're not making a move
to kill it, as pandas are highly endangered.
Maybe we should try making babies with it.
I read somewhere that, next to diamonds,
pandas are the hardest things to make on earth.

POSSUM DAWN

Everywhere this morning, dead possums. Bodies broken open, heads crushed, blood bursting out. One in a ditch, one at the intersection, one in the middle of the road. Their striped faces and black eyes look still alive. The farther we drive, the more we see. We never knew they were here. Surely this must be some kind of sign.

"Superstitious folk will bury an opossum head down so if it comes back to life, it'll keep digging instead of dragging itself to the surface to resume its life, as opossums are bold opportunists," today's newspaper reads under the headline, "The 'O' Is Always Silent."

were gone. In every empty tent,
beds were made. In the mess hall,
plates were clean and put away
and all the cabinets filled with full
boxes of sugary cereal. "Has this
happened before?" I asked Stan. He
just shrugged, obviously disappointed.
We'd spent days preparing our speech,
charging our prods. "Someone
must've tipped them off," I said.
"Or some*thing*," Stan said, pulling
a spray bottle out of his backpack.
I cut the lights and stepped away
as he spritzed the wall and words
arose like ghosts: WE PRETENDED
TO BE DUMB   Stan stared at it
awhile. "Do you know how to read?"
"No, but you gotta *love* that luminol!"

VISITING UNCLE J IN KING COUNTRY

His hand shakes as he ashes out the cracked window,
breaking 75 on hairpin two-lane blacktop lined with
"Life's a gift" billboards facing backward on both sides.
Whose gaffe's that? Maybe the signs are pointed at
grain-silo security cams topping each little gray hill.
Bare trees lining the Big Sioux look like smoke, but the air
billowing from the Blue Bunny factory reeks of ice cream.
We pass the farmhouse he lived in with a hippie young
enough to be his daughter. "They let it go to hell!" he haws
and guns it. Next time we visit, let's check out the Loess Hills.
Here and China are the only places we'll ever see something
like that. Real pretty. "Are you coming in June?" we ask
when he drops us off at the hotel. "If I live that long!"
He coughs (he didn't) and peels out. Across from mounds
of sand dragged from the river, bound in orange plastic nets,
the blinking casino looks like a giant squid signaling at
something. Not us. And that two-step bar behind
the casino? Fake. I can't prove it. I just know.

THE DAY AFTER THE FAIR

a drone discovered the sea of dead
but the people back at HQ piloting the drone
were dead, too—their bodies crumpled
on a deep-blue carpet—so the drone
flew till its battery ran out and plummeted
into the endless, undulating hills of dead
people, pork chops on a stick, garbage . . .
Some protein had come gunning for us
and the Spin Out flung it everywhere.
Efficient. It happened slowly over

millions of years. It happened in
an instant. The mushroom spores blown in
to break down the plastic and people made it
to the soundboard, tripped the loudspeakers,
and flooded the dead world with the Band
singing "When I Paint My Masterpiece,"
which the mushrooms loved and learned to sing
just like Levon. The spores memorized all the songs
and books and pictures—thought these were
lists of things we wanted bad but never got.

CRUSHING IT

I don't wanna brag but I'm pretty sure
I got the highest score ever on the ADHD test.
The best part was when Mike asked me to juggle
a hatchet, a balloon full of pudding, and a hamster,
and I was all, "Hold my beer, Mike!" Okay . . .
I tanked it. I could go pro at wrong. Blur—
I mean blue—ribbon wrong. You know that
feeling: you're throwing elbows like nobody's
business but when you finally get up to the window,
you can't sign your name right, and the teller gets
to keep your money? Which is not
legal in ANY state, Mike assures me.
Thank you, Mike (if that is
your real name).

SONG OF THE HUMMING DRUMLINS

Should I turn around to *get,* to *get*—
no, to *return* the ice cubes I found in my pocket
to the freezer? No. Keep going.

When I finally make it to the ocean
I realize:

1) My toes have been too close
2) to the edge of the pier, and
3) my aunt Marilyn isn't really ignoring
4) my growing list of accomplishments,
5) she's dead. About ten years now.

Dead and ignoring are kind of the same
superhero power, whereas dragging
that fifty-foot hose for miles as I'd been
doing was just all-alone dumb.

I pulled my pockets inside out, ad infinitum.
No one living tried to stop me from dragging
that hose down the street to the ocean,
but the dead waved their arms and howled
from atop the dotted yellow line.
Cars plowed right through 'em.

The ocean *is* nice. I should come here
more often. The phone rings. It's Marilyn
and her voice is *so, so, so*—no,
happy for me.

MY MOTHER VISITS ME IN PRISON

"I was in prison once!" she chirps, as if it's a story
about winning the lottery. "Really?" I ask, unsure
if she's lying on purpose or her brain's hiding
the truth from her like the queen in a game
of three-card monte. "Where'd the red lady land?"
her brain asks, revealing three cards upside down,
blue-and-white backs depicting flowery thickets
through which no light passes. It'll be impossible
for her to pick. "This game's rigged," I whisper,
tug at her sleeve, but she's already closed her eyes—
her pupils carom beneath see-through lids. The family
next to us begins to cry. All of them. They hold one
another's hands across the table. The guard barks,
they unhand and cry harder, there's no release, only
a bottomless well of grief. My mother stares.
"That orange bird sings such a pretty song!"

CHARLIE VESTAL'S MEMORIAL SERVICE

You'd show up in pajama pants and slippers
to dig ditches for the old boy at the mic.
He knew you'd always be an hour late,
and then you'd have to go get breakfast,
which took another hour, then another hour
to eat it. Laughter. "Tomorrow, Charlie,
please wear boots," old boy says he'd beg.
Some cry. So many people wanted you safe
and dry. Old boy thanks us all and steps aside
for Auntie, next in line, who remembers you
finally in your own apartment, getting it
together. Look how loved you were!
This place is packed! Janie, in the ER
with her daughter all last night, hasn't slept
in thirty-six hours. "I had to come." What a funny
way to meet someone: after they're dead.
Your light's still pulling grins from glowing
faces though it's gone, slipped into the next
song. Later, alone in the car, I tell myself, "Be
kind. Be kind. Be kind. Be kind. Be kind."

JOY

Abby hates car rides. All buck and thrash,
    her gray swayback swells and her limbs
flail like drumsticks when we lift her
    ("One, two, three!") into the backseat.
Hey, if I'd spent ten years in a cage
    same size as my body having babies,
a liquid world whipping by on all sides
    would make me puke, too. She stands stiff
as a dead beehive the whole ride, toppling
    into turns, crumpling onto her face at stop-
lights. But yesterday, first nice day in months,
    you decided to drive all the dogs to the lake.
It's a hoot to watch them chase whiffs of scat.

    "Hold Abby on your lap so she can stick her
nose out the window," you said in the car
    because you don't believe in coddling things,
especially the frightened if fright's gone.
    I held her by the harness in case she spooked,
kissed her on the head, rubbed her ears, gently
    felt the last tooth—her sunken muzzle's sharp surprise.
She kept her nose pointed into the wind and

    blinked. Her muscles began to melt, she started
slipping, but I propped her back up. At the lake,
    the other dogs ran far enough ahead to see
us and be seen, but Abby just stood there,
    eyes locked—"Don't you move"—
(maybe she was worried about finding her way
    home if we dumped her) so she missed
the swirling, sqwonking flock of rosy birds as they
    landed fifty feet away. The other dogs froze:
"What the fuh—"

"Those are pelicans!" I yelled,
because someone had recently told me pelicans
        migrate through Iowa, and I'd thought,
"You're a liar. I'll never see such a thing."
        "Look, Abby!" we said and pointed at the wobbly
weirdos chasing freaked-out geese behind her,
        but Abby distrusted our laughter and its source.
Joy was a strange bird she'd never trust
        or try to catch.

ABBY, THE COMEDIAN

I'm surprised how long it takes
her heart to stop. Strong old girl. Dr. Murrell
keeps the stethoscope pressed to her ribs.
I lean down in front of her unblinking eyes.

"You're a good dog, Abby," I assure her.
Deb, Denny, and Dr. Murrell agree. "You *are*
a good dog, Abby." A beat or two . . . he puts
the stethoscope away. Faint gray spots on her

rump I've never noticed. Did they swim up
when she got sick? No, I remember hearing color
begins in the skin. Denny coughs. "This is
the saddest one—she had a hard life."

"Found love in the end, though," Dr. Murrell says,
looking down, petting her, and it's true.
If Abby's life had been a Greek play, technically
it would've been a comedy—but how does

Dr. Murrell know that? Can he feel it through her
still-warm hide, shooting off hairs with each pass?
Denny scoops her up and carries her to the truck.
Her stuck-out white paw bounces with each step—

Bye-bye. Bye-bye. Bye-bye. Back at the house,
we wait for Collin to help Denny dig the hole.
"Dr. Murrell seems like a nice guy," I say, and (I think
to let me know Dr. Murrell wasn't blowing smoke

or maybe to make me feel better) Denny says,
"Dr. Murrell knew everything about her."

MARILYN, EVERY DAY WE WONDER

what you'd think about all this. I imagine
you crashing through the inaugural barricades
or flying a stolen helicopter into a wildfire
with a margarita gripped between your knees.
Remember, gridlocked on the 5, you winked
at a bearded dude leaning on the asphalt roller
(I'd only seen women wink at men in movies),
he leered ("I might get laid!") and you drawled,
"Why don't you get that piece of shit out of the road?"
Shock splashed across his face. "Lock the doors!"
"Crazy bitch!" he roared and punched our hood,
clueless how close he was to getting his ass shot.
We found the loaded gun under your mattress:
Smith & Wesson, cowgirl style, swirly pearl handle,
and the serial number filed off. We like to take it
out at parties. "What a cute gun!" We also found
several transistor radios and a box of old weed.
Cheers, Auntie. With one phone call, you scared
my scary Brooklyn landlord into fixing my dead bolt.
You were six states away and a seventy-two-year-old
woman! There's a pack of kids down the street in a house
that's falling apart. We never see an adult. No matter
how cold or dark it is, they're always playing outside
with a new puppy. We have no idea where the old
puppies have gone, but if you were here, we know
there'd be no more of this New Puppy bullshit.

NAME THAT TUNE

Lately my eighty-four-year-old mother's been
hearing noises: a party in the street below
her bedroom window—gruff men cursing,
a woman's laugh, a scream, beer cans dinking
off the concrete. When she finally got the nerve
to peek out, nothing but a streetlight. Sounds
coming from inside her, she says. Pops, clicks,
swooshes, gongs, alarms, heavy steps pounding
through her as if someone's stumbling around
on the roof. Her cell phone rings. "Hello?" No
answer from its flat, gray face. Pounding on
the door she never used to lock, so hard she feared
the wood would split, but the peephole: empty.
A voice in the middle of the night: "Jo*ann!*"—
impatient to get her attention. "That must be
terrifying," I said. She giggled, "It was something!
You know that poem, 'I Sing the Body Electric'?"
"Of course. Did you recognize the voice?" I asked.
"It must've been *my* mother because she called me
Jo*ann!*"— she imitated her mother's scolding voice—
"in just *that* way." "A woman?" I asked. "Yes.
A stranger might call me Jody." "Yes,
so, at least it's someone who knows you."

MEETING MYRON FLOREN

Big Red could've had any woman under the beer tent, that hot Polish Fest afternoon—skirts swirling atop the slamming gams of octogenarian polka groupies. At eighty-one, he was still all man and so cool. I'll never be that cool. His boss, Lawrence Welk, was certainly not that cool. Lawrence always looked purple to me, like he'd been screaming at the Lennon Sisters during the Mutual of Omaha commercial. I've never wanted kids, but I wanted Myron to make me pregnant. I waited hours in the autograph line, up to my waist in blue hair. His fans didn't want to speed things along. When I finally made it to the front, there he was: tan, grinning, a cold, golden beer in his hand, his wavy hair still streaked with red. I'm talking total dynamite . . . but—

"What happened to your rings?!" I blurted—all his pimptastic bling flashing Morse code as his hands bounded over the accordion keys like a roided-out Russian gymnast. Myron answered to the crowd, "An old friend got robbed leaving a gig, but the robbers couldn't get his ring off, so they took his finger—" the fans gasped. Myron grinned and *winked at me* [!] which flushed a bursting sweat-bead down my ass crack. "And that's why I don't wear 'em anymore!" "Hooray!" the crowd cheered. "Good call!" someone shouted, and everyone laughed, except me—the goon who couldn't tell a body or its wake from the glitz it's shed.

WRAPPING UP THE TIME-SHARE SEMINAR

So we could look upon the lies
I've told you all as one would
sheep [slide: sheep]. Sheep gotta
eat, that's rule number one, so you find
a quiet field with some unsullied grass
[slide: grassy field] and let them do
their thing. And here's the thing: they
do go do their thing—every time!
That's proof of something [slide:
scientific symbols flying around].

Living—and I'm talking the basic stuff
here like eating and coming in out
of the rain [slide: donkey in rain]—
requires a suspension of disbelief:
"I'm eating this tofu for my *Tomorrow* Me."
And that's charming, kind of [slide:
charm bracelet with sheep charms]:
these job-masks made of lies are lovely-
dumb things on our faces [big smile]!

Can we help it? Maybe . . . or we *could*
look upon the lies as gifts from ghosts
[slide: Casper] who know too well the
formlessness awaiting us, that decisions
are illusions [slide: rabbit in a black top hat]
of the ego. The only real thing's the real
wind scooping our skulls out
[slide: sunset view of the Badlands].

                    Thank you!

TOURISTS

Mardi Gras World made us feel like we were on
acid. "Let's ride the ferry," you say. Shake it off.
The terminal's enormous and empty but for us
and that other person: ambiguously wrapped
in a cop-blue parka, thick scarf up to the sunglasses,
wool hat, legs stuck straight out in a folding chair
next to a space heater plugged into a faraway socket
by a chain of cords, white-orange-black, hooked
tooth to tail. Across the river, Algiers Point must be more
than its few roofs let on to have warranted this grand
ingress—steel now a-rash in peeling paint. Our ferry
nearly clips a paddleboat flying a frilly Swamp Tour flag.
Passengers slosh pink drinks. "Whoa!" The ferry head-
butts tires tied to the dock until it's close enough to stick
out a red gangplank. First off, a man in a shapeless,
sun-bleached suit, blue paper shoes, bagless IV pole
in one hand and a long unlit [*fwip*] lit cigarette in the other,
followed by a fast, frowning woman, black-lined lips,
flip-flops and short shorts despite the record lows. Then
we're on the other side! Just like that! An unremarkable
crossing, but when we hit town ground, I look around . . .
"Why's everyone white?" It hadn't been so since Iowa.
"Dunno." We order beers in Jack's Shack down the hill.
"Where y'all from?" "Gotta pee." I lock myself in a stall
and google "Algiers Point." Photos after Katrina taken
from the shore right outside, of white people shooting
at everyone else swimming across the river, fleeing
over the bridge. "Drink up!" I say, interrupting the barfly
schooling you on crackheads. "'Cause it stinks?" you ask,
and it hits me: a smell viler than bile, sugarier than shat pants
oozing from underneath us: a below-sea-level basement
or crawl space. I give you a too-little nod to let you know
my "yes" is big. On our way back, another couple exits a bar.

"Hey." Tourists, too, from Florida, a father and daughter
who look nothing alike: she's Cher with a tiny nose, pumped
for Harrah's Zeppelin tribute, belting out "The Crunge."
A karaoke ringer, no doubt. Dad, rocking a pompadour
like a Hindu James Brown, is all about roulette and
a daiquiri. Me too! We talk about what we're going to
eat next. You moan, "I'm still full from last night!"
This concerns the dad. "Noooo," he scolds, urging
you to hear him for real. "You gotta *eat*. Something
with cornmeal that sticks to you, son.
You gotta keep your strength up."

II. Ours

FINDING A DRAWER FULL OF DRIVER'S LICENSES:

*The Golden State Killer stole "trophies" from his victims such
as flatware, jewelry, photographs, and driver's licenses. Twenty
years after his crime spree stopped, police began to release lists of
missing items in hopes that someone—a family member, a home
health aide—would recognize an item and report the owner,
who would then be in his eighties. In a statement to the public,
a detective said, "If you find a drawer full of driver's licenses at
your uncle's house, call us."*

All expired. Mostly women, in their 30s
when the photos were taken. Now they'd be
in their 60s and 70s. A few men frowning
under uneven mustaches. Some faces scratched
out to white blurs in the plastic. How funny
was fashion back then? Pointy collars wide
as wind socks, all that argyle, hard hair,
eyeglasses so thick—why, it'd be like peering
out of the freezer through the narrowing
window of ice. Back then nothing defrosted
itself—they babysat their appliances, untethered
their thick black cords from the walls and
waited till the water ran off wherever it wanted—
unmarked Tupperware and ice trays left behind.

IRWIN ALLEN VS. THE LION TAMER

We used to love lion tamers because people really didn't know
who would win in a battle of man versus nature. Back then
all the stories ended in death, our death, by mauling or snakebite
or dog bite or being struck by lightning, smothered by an avalanche,
charged off a cliff, carried away in the talons of an eagle, inhaled
by a whale, stung by a scorpion, swarmed by killer bees, gored
by a rhino, poisoned by berries, pricked by a sticker, swallowed
by quicksand, beguiled by a black cat, gobbled by a witch—

So imagine the relief: with one flick of the whip and an "Up!"
the skulking lion stands on legs like a human. Its toothy protest,
no big thing. After all those years of fear, I'd laugh at it, too,
and that's what people did until there were no more lions
to laugh at, but Irwin Allen knew death doesn't live in a thing
you can kill with a gun. It's not the heat—it's the hubris. The fire
that wipes the city out begins in birthday candles and the happy
huff behind them. The storm that flips the cruise ship starts
in the sea that rises up to fill the empty sky. An airplane crash
begins not in birds but in the feeders we've stolen the seed from,
certain nobody can see us.

PRETTY

A head taller but a year younger than my girlfriends
with their bouncy boobs and full-blown rosebushes.
They knew how to squeeze into tight white zip-around
jeans without getting their pubes snagged in the metal
teeth, clenched from tag to belly button. You couldn't
wear underwear with those things. My tight white jeans
were too short and gave me a camel toe—my clit
popped like a knuckle against the seam. In skates, I was
even taller, hunched, mouth agape or talking shit, squinting,
always this close to falling, flailing, arms out, neck-deep
in an incoming tide. I couldn't skate sideways or backward,
or even fast, so when the lights dimmed, and the disco ball
lit up, and the boy on black skates (the slick kind
you couldn't rent at the rink) with red toe stops
rolled up and held out his hand, I—

                                    "He's asking you
to skate!" my girlfriend said. "Duh, dumbass!" hawed
another, hard, as she pushed me from behind. I took his hand
and he gently—in a way that showed he knew I couldn't skate—
led me into the current. "(Nobody Gets) Too Much Heaven"
by the Bee Gees. I looked down at my flabby little tits, all
nipple, not at the boy with blond hair I'd seen at the rink
before, skating for hours (backward, jumps) but always
alone. I felt sorry for him, until I looked up and realized
he was much older than me . . . and all the kids around us.
The song ended. He asked me to skate again and I said,
"No, I'm tired," but thought, "You must think I'm pretty
fucking stupid," which is exactly the same thing I think
now, whenever a stranger holds his hand out to me.

DOE STORIES

The brain is hardwired for stories—so much so
that if the story's told backward or in a language
we can't speak, the brain still knows it's a story.
Suppose on the news you see a truck driver say
he was just poking around an illegal dump site
on his lunch break and found an old TV console,
the kind that made TVs look like furniture, drywall
nailed to the front and back where the TV used to be.
He kicked it over, the boards broke off, and a metal
suitcase spilled out. He kicked that, too. Inside:
a black plastic bag containing the body of a child,
he judged by the size, curled in a fetal position.
Now let's say scientists take you into a room and you
tell them this story on videotape. Then they play that
tape to a stranger. The truck driver, the scientists,
the stranger, and you: all your brains align in a cognitive
eclipse—brains of people you haven't met yet and may
never meet (like the detective, twenty years later, re-
constructing the child's face from a few baby teeth)
can't wait to hear how this story turns out.

THE NEW IQ TEST

Fences: do you see them
or through them—
like if a dog came
running at you,
would you know to run?

Math: how many rabbits
need to see a rabbit torn apart
to know there's a fence there?
If just one rabbit, can you,
the living rabbit, chill
behind the real fence?

Pointing: do your eyes
follow a finger to the prey?

Mirrors: yes, hell
no, or hell?

Tupperware: can you
make it with your hands?
Anything plastic ought to be
free to those who will initiate
the breakdown process.

Free: do you remember
when it was, or was it ever?
Never. You see now, no,
know the tide's always been
pulling away like a contour sheet
with spent elastic. Maybe
it's just tired of holding
on to the fence.

#DONNERPARTY #THOUGHTSANDPRAYERS

July 4, 1846. The scouts who'd made it back
over Hastings Cutoff scanned our clan like a far-
off copse of junipers through supper's grace,
ate standing up without chewing, and passed
on our fireside fiddle. Those men were humming
at a different frequency—like cicadas, high and
throbbing—perhaps too high for Uncle Jim to hear,
for when they warned him, "Go right," over a road
he'd only seen on paper, he whooped, "Every
animal's got enough brains to tan its own hide!"
and we thought, "Well . . . what the hell? Some-
one has to feel like they know what's what,"
because we were humming at the slower, low-
er frequency of soon-to-vanish oxen.

WHITE PEOPLE DAY

Damn it feels good to be individual together!
The line for the fun house was so long it wiped
out our memory of how we came to be here.
Inside, the mirrors were all single-serving size,
emphasizing our selves, you see? I'm, you're,
we're all uniquely single-minded, wearing T-shirts
with the name of the world's highest-grossing
movie on them. My boy points, "Daddy, what
are those things floating over the mountain?"
"New soft-serve flavors, son! The end!" I declare,
but they turn out to be "hat are buroons."
When we shot holes in their puffed-up breasts,
they sang songs called "uhlarms" or so
said the animals driving them.

GUINEA PIGS

are Andean rodents that were originally
     domesticated for food, then imported
to Europe as pets for rich people.
     Queen Elizabeth I had a pet guinea pig.
The oldest guinea pig skeleton in England
     dates back to 1540. Imagine: guinea pigs
traveling all that way by boat, which were, back
     then, dark and riddled with rot, stench, rats,
and scurvy, King Killer of Nutritional Deficiencies,
     which out-killed other nutritional deficiencies
by attacking the one thing connecting
     everything in our bodies: collagen, a Greek
word derived from the practice of boiling
     down horse parts for glue. Guinea pigs
were eventually used as guinea pigs
     in early experiments on scurvy, which moved
through them and broke them down much
     the same way it did us. It was about time. The rats
we'd been using in the labs—something
     about their fleas, which seemingly knew no
bounds—had started to give us the willies.

CAKE IN PARLOUR

The butler bent down to scratch his bald head hard
on a gold-brocade pillow depicting a fox hunt: dogs'
teeth flashing, slashing the shy beast's flesh. "Tuggly!"
the dowager yelped, then bent down to scratch her own
head on a pillow showing haloed hunters hoisting a bloody
stag's heart heavenward. "WILL WE HAVE ENOUGH
PILLOWS?" I had to holler, as the hysterical giggling phase
had commenced. Auntie snorted boredly, but lit up as the maid
brought out brains resembling Swiss cheese . . . full of holes.
"IS IT OKAY TO EAT THESE?" I asked. Undaunted, Auntie
snatched one off the tray and plunged her finger knuckle-
deep into a hole. "WE CAN HIDE BULLETS IN HERE!"
she roared, slurping her finger in and out, her chapped
lips pulsing with a million tiny stars.

FULL HOUSE

We'll never know the Tanners any better than we do
after the show's forty-two-second intro, when the girls come
dancing over a green San Francisco hill, laughing at a joke
we missed. A happy man strums a guitar, but we can't hear
his song because the intro's drowning him out (maybe
he's just moving his lips). Another man touches his car,
stares at the camera and smiles. That's all there is to know!
Which means we know the Tanners better than the real
people we love who are silently jettisoning thoughts and
parts of themselves that no longer benefit them, as a snake
sheds dead skin. Sometimes, that skin is us, and they don't
know they're changing, but we do, far before we're
sloughed off in the grass. The Tanners are like mushrooms:
born with every cell they need. No matter how
much it rains, they'll soak it up. Only the singers
of their theme song will ever change size.

CALIFORNIA HOBO INSURANCE

contains 500,000 pages on the ineligibility
of lottery winners, but keep reading because
golden Yosemite—and all its opportunities
to disappear without a trace and have your-
self declared legally dead—lies on the other side
where redwoods reek of briny formaldehyde.
You know that old kids' song about John Muir
marrying a tree? Fun fact: in the 1909 version, he
poops in all the park's trash cans, and the rangers
beat his ass till he's brain-damaged, but trail signs
suggest Muir had Authorization. Here's the plaque
(misspelled) rangers planted with his name
in the grass. So if you're traveling through
Yosemite, don't be nervous. [whispers] Some
of us are disappearing on purpose ;)

THE WINDOW IN THE MIRROR

"They know locks are important," the nurse says when she sees me watching a man, younger than my father, twist the switch of a dead bolt nailed to the wall in the dayroom—one of many locks nailed to the wall. Puzzles that can never be solved. Total fake-outs. A tumbler lock, a sliding-door latch, an interior doorknob with its little tongue sticking out . . .

At the table, a woman, also younger than my father, looms over two big piles of Christmas cards—her face frozen in a silent scream. The nurse explains the woman was in a car accident, and the part of her brain that manages fear got stuck on ON. Old Christmas cards are the only things that make her feel better.

The woman slowly picks up a card from the left-hand pile, opens it, closes it, then lays it down on the right-hand pile. Her fluid movement reminds me of a Japanese tea ceremony. A flimsy chain tethers her to the chair like a dog no one thinks will run away.

OH, THOSE NUTTY ZAGGERS

We gave the grumpy Luddite a new ax
to guard the power cables. [Whoops!
technical difficulties: national anthem,
Indian head] "Welcome back," snapped
the unwelcoming Welcome Wagon lady
setting up barricades, pouring concrete
abutments with the deaf dwarf director
of three-point free throws and musicals.
We asked the Human Torch to sign
the zero-hour stay of execution in wax.
"Keep it safe in your asbestos briefcase!"
we beseeched him. "Do you have any
fireworks?" he asked, totally not listening.
"Uh.................." We chose the sourest flour
for the Annual Come-Together Party cake,
which went untouched (too many grimy
hands and mouths on a knife at once =
rabies, baby), followed by a speech with no
words (just hunches & grunts) and corny
newsreels of the '48 cake. Velveeta noted
how lifelike its seemingly infinite tiers.

THIS IS A TERRIFIC POEM ABOUT ME BEING ELECTED PRESIDENT OF THE UNITED STATES. IT'S CALLED "COLOR ME TOMORROW, TODAY." [SHRUGS] THAT'S WEIRD, BUT IT'S REALLY A TERRIFIC POEM, FOLKS. THE *BEST*.

"Gird your loins, small-handed men . . ."
I like that. [hoots] "Strike up a wench-
pithy polka to which . . ." [eyes dart left,
makes stink face] ". . . teeeyooo wheech . . ."
[makes fey gesture with tiny hand, crowd
goes bananas] It's a poem, folks! [laughter]
Okay—okay, back to the poem: "For every goodly
man in this stadium here today, I say unto thee . . ."
[eye roll] It's like the fucking Bible [yee-haws]
"I am scared of new words and mirrors"?
"I am a trapped raccoon-man"?
What is this shit? [hands off poem
to giant glowing hairless toxic-waste baby
in the front row, baby eats the poem, glows
brighter] Lookit that! [points, crowd applauds,
caws, makes chain saw/machine gun sounds].
Now that's the power of poetry, folks! [cue
Charlie Rich: "(When We Get) Behind Closed Doors."
President ascends on wires.]

THE INTELLECTUALS OF MONGOLIA AND THEIR
INFLUENCE ON MODERN ART

"Please stop <u>stealing</u> my vegetables," says the cardboard sign
in my neighbor's zucchini patch, a zucchini patch that only exists
because I planted zucchini last year and seeds blew into his yard—
actually, the no-man's-land between our yards—I could probably find
a property map showing where the vines cross into our yard.

The zucchini are enormous: two feet long, five pounds each,
at least twenty of them out there. They will rot on the vines
because the neighbor's an idiot—he doesn't even know
what they are, which is why his sign doesn't say, "Please stop <u>stealing</u>
my zucchini." I saw him mowing the lawn once (his lawn is very
mowed): a young white man wearing a red polo shirt, tan pleated pants
and wraparound black sunglasses that made him look like a cyborg.

The curtains in his house are always drawn, which makes me think
he's cooking meth in there, and the American flag hanging next to his
front door makes me think he's racist. I'm going to make a sign and lay it
over his sign: "They're <u>zucchini</u>, asshat, and the only reason you need
that many giant ones is if you're swapping them out for sex toys." Then
I'm going to write the word "<u>micropenis</u>" on his car with a Sharpie,
just because.

I've been perusing privacy fences online. There are many kinds.
Some are quite creative. I miss New Yorkers' fear. If Iowans worried
100 percent more about getting beat up, there'd be no more signs,
and they'd tailgate less, too—that shit'll get you shot in New York.
I considered sharing my rage about the zucchini sign on Facebook,
but they're all on Facebook—posting pictures of their grandkids
and talking about Jesus—and it's too long for Twitter. I had to tell
someone, so I decided to hide it in a place they'd never look.

TODAY ON *UNTAMED IOWA,* "THE LAND OF THE BIG BALL HEAVERS"!

Their antlers are all rack, twelve points and up, so heavy
on their heads, every moment feels as if a hollow-
brained linebacker's rushing up to sack them in a rage
of barks and too-tight copper socks leaving marks.
Whoa! Have we already gone too far afield? Eaten too
much string to thread our way back to Foggy Marsh,
where big ball heavers roam? No, there they are: see
their soft ears perk as we approach, their pupils flush
and swallow their blue halos whole. Oo, that's not good
actually. They only do that when they're under water
or duress from beavers/beaver fever. Swing your stick
and shout, "SHOO!" Sing owly songs of heaving balls
to soothe them as they shoo!, of balls as big as buxom
Bundt cakes and their holes! Yodel in the holes as all
the big ball heavers flee, "Adieu, whitetails! Sorry
for your rapid hearts! Bye-bye, black iyee-iyee-eyes!"

THIS IS DEDICATED TO THE ONE I LOVE

We told ourselves we did it for the next room
over in the natural history museum—the roped-
off one they'd been hammering on forever—
but really we did it for the money, for money's
machinations that kept the crude rude and boiling.
The money was born a baby with our face [Aw!].
We sang to it and as it grew into a whirligig of gas spouts,
we sang louder, splitting into harmonies like air-show jets,
doo-wopping with our waists cinched in rubber bands
to hit the inhumane high notes. We laughed about it
at Mama Cass's backyard picnic (we laughed about
everything—it was *that* kind of picnic [winks]—we
were all really connected, you know? [exhales])
talking about the next shape clouds would shift
into. This was back when the baby had our face,
not our absence's, our unwinding's.

MY MOTHER VISITS ME IN PRISON, AGAIN

Hardwired for fear, I severed the snake's head
from the cord, but now the floodlights kick on
by themselves. I studied people in meetings:
listened, took notes. "Does anyone here speak
fluent oppositional defiant disorder? No? Hello?"

So imagine my surprise when I opened one eye,
saw the flower, and it filled me all the way to
the edges and felt good. "Get a mirror," it said.
I laughed, "No way." Suddenly a beautiful horse

was looking back at me. "I've been so badly
allergic to you," I said. Nothing happened next
or before. What a beautiful horse! Myopia,
au revoir! "Hey, Mom, come look at this,"
I called her. Slowly she opened one eye.

HERO

After ten years passed, all citizens were invited
to search for the body because police thought
we'd never find it, but I've lived here all my life.
I never knew the itch was a frozen part of me
paying attention until I could let it off the leash
alongside my dog, who knew everything I knew
but none of the nonsense—this made him our boss.
If you tell them you know something unknowable
they'll think you did it. After thinking "She's here"
for a year and she wasn't, I could've kept on being
wrong, but I caught a cold that lasted all winter.
What to make of that? Our first trip back out, the dog
whined at a different turn. Is he not a citizen?
Here's something: but for a few branches broken
under ice, the wrong field mirrored the right.

FACELIFT

I met the woman whom I hadn't seen in years
at a bar with many happy friends around her.
I could tell right away she was different:
flushed as a flower, showing more leg—
and what legs!—smiling with her teeth apart,
breathless as if she'd just run her first
marathon and someone kind had thrown
a shiny silver blanket over her shoulders.
"I'm getting a divorce," she said, tugging down
the corners of her grin like a too-short skirt,
"it's a hard time," she looked away. "But
a little exciting, right?" I asked, remembering
the relief: not knowing what would happen
next, but knowing what would never again:
my begging to be loved the way I thought
I could but had no proof. What he said
didn't exist: I was all the proof I needed.

PASSION OF THE POLLINATORS

The Russian sage bush in the driveway's gone
berserko, shooting shoots like fireworks,
some ten feet long, in all directions. Oh,
and the whole thing smells like BO. Go
figure: flora rivaling Disney's froofiest princess
reeks like teenage pits. Green-gray frilly stalks
droop under all the bewitched bumblebees rocking
the pollen-packed purple flower-clusters, stems
swayback beneath their unbuckable buzz. The bees
have dumped a thick carpet of petals onto the concrete
in the same shape as the bush's undulating shadow—
a purple shadow peppered with a few dead bees.
The shadow's a portrait the bees painted of their love,
a painting worth dying for, titled, *This. Shit. Right. Here.*
When I walk by, they follow close as if to say, "Keep
walkin', bozo." After dark, they're sleeping sheep in it.
My headlights glint off their black unblinking eyes.

ODE TO YOUR HYPERVIGILANCE

Hugging you is hard enough when you're awake,
but to worm my arm under your downed trunk,
plutonium-core sequoia, and hold on? *Pft*.
Not with electric jolts reanimating your limbs in
spurts, flinches, clinches, kicks, *grrr*s—I'm bucked
off. All night, these seismic pulses. Where's the
firefight, honey? Perhaps beyond the gun range's
gate at the end of the gravel road behind our house.
Every shot *boom-pop*s the air and our little dogs
slink around with folded ears. So much for a nice
summer stroll. "Those yahoos," you growl,
"shoot at empty chairs."

GETTING A WAX FROM MARISOL

She tells me about giving herself a Brazilian
when she was nine months pregnant.
"Girl, you should be the fucking president,"
I want to say, but instead I stick with
"You did not." "I did! I was like . . ."
she mimes tunneling up her butt cheeks—
"where's the top of this thing?!"

THE RABIES SONG

At the bar, a rabies expert says
     there are places on this planet
        with no rabies.

          "Are they small and surrounded
            by water?" I want to ask but
               don't want to interrupt.

Shots were a game-changer in the '50s, apparently.

"When my mom was a little girl, kids would yell,
     'Mad dog!' and everyone would scatter.
        Now for no reason, she likes to shout, 'Mad dog!'"
          I say, and laugh, but the expert

shakes her head, "Rabies was
           and *is* a big deal."

"Can birds get rabies?"

    "No!" she swats the question out of the air.

"What *can* get rabies?"

    "Any mammal!" she snaps and
        the crowd *Whoooo*s. More people
          at the bar are listening in because
            we're talking about rabies.

"A giraffe?"

"Never seen a case, but I'm sure it's happened!"

"A raccoon?"

"Sure! And they'll rip you apart!" she gestures.
"Oh, boy! I bet!"

"Run right up your leg!" she adds.

"Their little hands!"
someone shouts.

"What about a rabid bear?" I ask

and wow—I wish you could've heard
the crowd with their beers cheer for the bear,
seen the expert nodding deeply
and her husband cracking up . . .

Our roar was like a corny song I'd always
rolled my eyes at, but now it was so old—
like a taxidermied dodo—it felt good
to sing along with everyone in the bar,
and though I'd never sung the song before,

I knew all the words—apparently
I'd absorbed them, just by living so long.

POETRY EVERYWHERE

Above the window in the dentist's office,
through which I watch sparrows pop around
the branches of a white-light-laced pine tree—
is that where the poetry is?—a man on TV says,
"Our president is a liar." *That's not where
the poetry is, is it?* "Can I have nitrous?" I ask,
a tear teetering. *Is that where the poetry is?*
"Bad experiences?" she asks. *There?* "Very."
"You bite the inside of your cheeks in your sleep,"
she notes, looking inside me with a light. "I tear
myself apart," I strain my jaw to share the scars.
Maybe there? "I would give it to you, but I can't
be near nitrous. Just took a pregnancy test. I don't
want anyone to know, so. Let's reschedule
you with someone else," she winks. *There
it is.* "Of course . . . Congratulations."

EVERY MAN A KING

Through his diamond-encrusted abalone-shell
binoculars, Jack London watches Huey P. Long
scramble down the terraced vineyard, built in the style
of rice paddies Jack'd observed in Japan while hunting
rare dwarf bears there. The whole mountain took fifty
men and a million clams to complete. Worth every penny,
Jack thinks as he watches Huey stumble down a hill, ripping
out rows of withered vines with the shotgun he's brought.
Jack chortles and accidentally swallows his opium lozenge.
Their duel was set for noon, but Jack knows by the *whoosh*
of wing-stirred air tickling his ear hairs that buzzards have
already spotted Huey on his back, his once-white suit now
besmirched. Ravens would follow . . . cougars. "Jack!" his wife
calls from the driver's seat of an idling tractor, the most
expensive tractor in the world. "Goddamn! How did you
get it running?" he asks. "Tits!" she pips with a shrug,
and spits. Jack saw, in the fog of her otherness, the
future changing shape: a neon lasso deftly twirled.

EFFIGY MOUNDS NATIONAL MONUMENT, IOWA

Before there was the time we see
there was the time we saw through,
when the biggest bear lay down,
exhaled the boundary of herself—
woof!—and rolled onto her side.

Her family followed in a line,
bending like an oxbow lake,
crocheting holes in the land
where water bubbled through
(so much does bubble through).

Birds saw the bears
bubbling up and dug it.
Whoa!

So with wing-fingers wide,
they pressed their feathered breasts
flat to the ground, which sang
their own songs back at them but
way slower, like whale
songs in
amber.

Is that a yes or a no? the birds asked.
Yes, replied the ground.
Whoa!

Green grass grew over them,
which was a long, green love song.

Nearby, turtles, panthers, dogs
lost their boundaries . . . exhaled . . . then

found them again and became
constellations.

What speed was the time
signature singing then when all those
holes in space opened up
and bear after bear,
bird after bird,
sun after sun lost, re-
found their shapes in
the long song, knowing
themselves at last for
what they were:

eternal,
immutable,
from every possible angle.

ACKNOWLEDGMENTS

Academy of American Poets' Imagine Your Parks: "Effigy Mounds National Monument, Iowa"

Academy of American Poets Poem-a-Day: "Name That Tune"

The American Poetry Review: "Doe Stories," "Guinea Pigs," "How to Manage Your Adult ADHD," "Old Women Talking about Death," "Wolverine Season," "You look at, not through, the window"

Bennington Review: "Marilyn, Every Day We Wonder"

Berfrois: "Irwin Allen vs. the Lion Tamer," "The New IQ Test," "Today on *Untamed Iowa,* 'The Land of the Big Ball Heavers'!"

Conduit: "Friend of the Devil," "The Morning I Met My New Family," "Posted: No Fledging in the Parking Lot"

Fence: "#donnerparty #thoughtsandprayers," "Possum Dawn"

Granta: "Full House," "My Mother Visits Me in Prison"

Hysterical: "Facelift," "The Rabies Song"

The Journal: "Hero"

jubilat: "Monochrome Rainbows"

Kenyon Review: "Finding a Drawer Full of Driver's Licenses:"

Lumina: "Wrapping Up the Time-Share Seminar"

Mississippi Review: "The Day after the Fair," "Joy"

New Limestone Review: "Meeting Myron Floren"

Nomadic Journal: "Ode to Your Hypervigilance," "Passion of the Pollinators"

Open Letters Monthly: "Crushing It," "Poetry Everywhere"

Ploughshares: "Abby, the Comedian," "The Gift," "This Is a Terrific Poem about Me Being Elected President of the United States. It's Called 'Color Me Tomorrow, Today.' [shrugs] That's Weird, but It's Really a Terrific Poem, Folks. The *Best,*" "The Window in the Mirror"

Poetry: "Mr. Big"

Spork: "California Hobo Insurance," "Every Man a King," "Oh, Those Nutty Zaggers," "Visiting Uncle J in King Country," "Zone 9: All the Village Idiots"

SWWIM Every Day: "Getting a Wax from Marisol"

Tupelo Quarterly: "Charlie Vestal's Memorial Service"

Typo: "Home Is Where the Mushrooms Grow," "This Is Dedicated to the One I Love"

WSQ: "The Intellectuals of Mongolia and Their Influence on Modern Art"

Zócalo Public Square: "Ode to Your Hypervigilance," "Song of the Humming Drumlins"

Thank you, thank you, thank you for your invaluable contribution to this book: Collin Switzer, Ada Limón and Jason Schneiderman, Barbara Ching, Erin Belieu, Alan Michael Parker, Laura Louise Minor, Larassa Kabel, the Iowa Arts Council, all the poets, and the folks at Copper Canyon Press.

Jennifer L. Knox is the author of four other collections of poetry: *Days of Shame and Failure* (2015), *The Mystery of the Hidden Driveway* (2010), *Drunk by Noon* (2007), and *A Gringo Like Me* (2005), all from Bloof Books. Her poems have appeared in the *American Poetry Review, Best American Erotic Poems, Granta, Great American Prose Poems, McSweeney's,* the *New York Times,* the *New Yorker,* and five times in the *Best American Poetry* series. She is the recipient of fellowships from the Iowa Arts Council and the Milwaukee County Arts Fund. Jennifer teaches at Iowa State University and is the proprietor of a small spice-blend company called Saltlickers.

Poetry is vital to language and living. Since 1972, Copper Canyon Press has published extraordinary poetry from around the world to engage the imaginations and intellects of readers, writers, booksellers, librarians, teachers, students, and donors.

WE ARE GRATEFUL FOR THE MAJOR SUPPORT PROVIDED BY:

THE PAUL G. ALLEN
FAMILY FOUNDATION

4
CULTURE

Anonymous
Jill Baker and Jeffrey Bishop
Anne and Geoffrey Barker
Donna and Matthew Bellew
Will Blythe
John Branch
Diana Broze
John R. Cahill
The Beatrice R. and Joseph A. Coleman Foundation Inc.
The Currie Family Fund
Laurie and Oskar Eustis
Austin Evans
Saramel Evans
Mimi Gardner Gates
Linda Fay Gerrard
Gull Industries Inc. on behalf of William True
The Trust of Warren A. Gummow
Carolyn and Robert Hedin
Bruce Kahn
Phil Kovacevich and Eric Wechsler

TO LEARN MORE ABOUT UNDERWRITING
COPPER CANYON PRESS TITLES,
PLEASE CALL 360-385-4925 EXT. 103

WE ARE GRATEFUL FOR THE MAJOR SUPPORT PROVIDED BY:

Lakeside Industries Inc. on behalf of Jeanne Marie Lee
Maureen Lee and Mark Busto
Peter Lewis and Johnna Turiano
Ellie Mathews and Carl Youngmann as The North Press
Larry Mawby and Lois Bahle
Hank and Liesel Meijer
Jack Nicholson
Gregg Orr
Petunia Charitable Fund and adviser Elizabeth Hebert
Gay Phinny
Suzanne Rapp and Mark Hamilton
Adam and Lynn Rauch
Emily and Dan Raymond
Jill and Bill Ruckelshaus
Cynthia Sears
Kim and Jeff Seely
Joan F. Woods
Barbara and Charles Wright
Caleb Young as C. Young Creative
The dedicated interns and faithful volunteers
of Copper Canyon Press

The Chinese character for poetry is made up
of two parts: "word" and "temple."
It also serves as pressmark for
Copper Canyon Press.

This book is set in Cardea.
Display type set in Knockout.
Book design by Gopa & Ted2, Inc.
Printed on archival-quality paper.